MW01625237

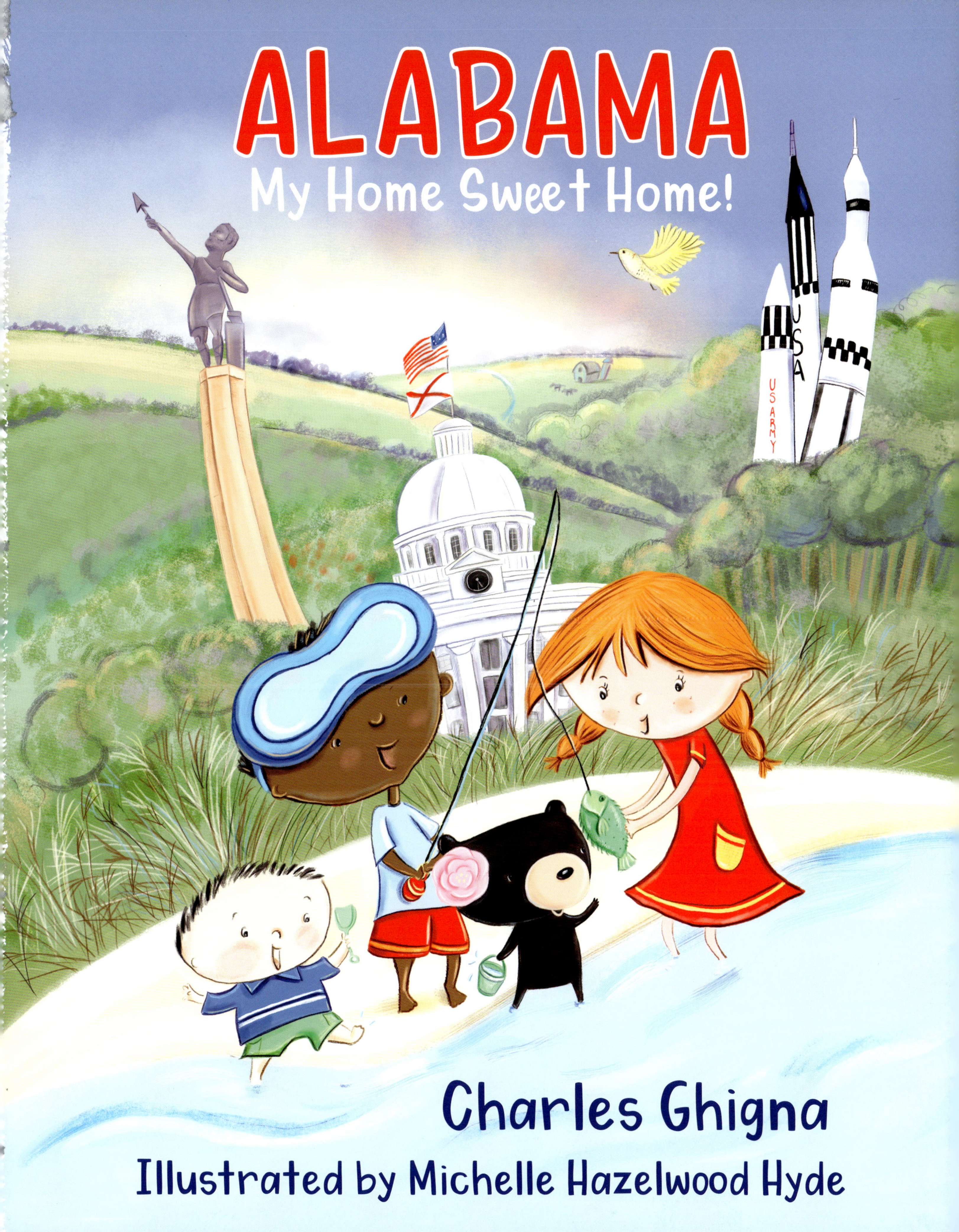
ALABAMA
My Home Sweet Home!
USA
US ARMY
Charles Ghigna
Illustrated by Michelle Hazelwood Hyde

ALABAMA
My Home Sweet Home!

Correspondence concerning this book may be directed to Whitman Publishing,
Attn: *ALABAMA: My Home Sweet Home!*, at the address above.

ISBN: 0794846513
PRINTED IN CHINA

ALABAMA
My Home Sweet Home!

By Charles Ghigna
Illustrated by Michelle Hazelwood Hyde

For the children of Alabama

Alabama My Home Sweet Home
is a journey through Alabama from Huntsville to the Gulf.

Our narrator is Camellia, a little Alabama black bear
cub who wears a camellia in her hair.

The Alabama black bear is our official state mammal
and the camellia is our official state flower.

The yellowhammer on the cover is our official state bird.

Alabama Celebration!
200 years in the nation.
From the mountains of Mentone
To the shores of Mobile Bay!

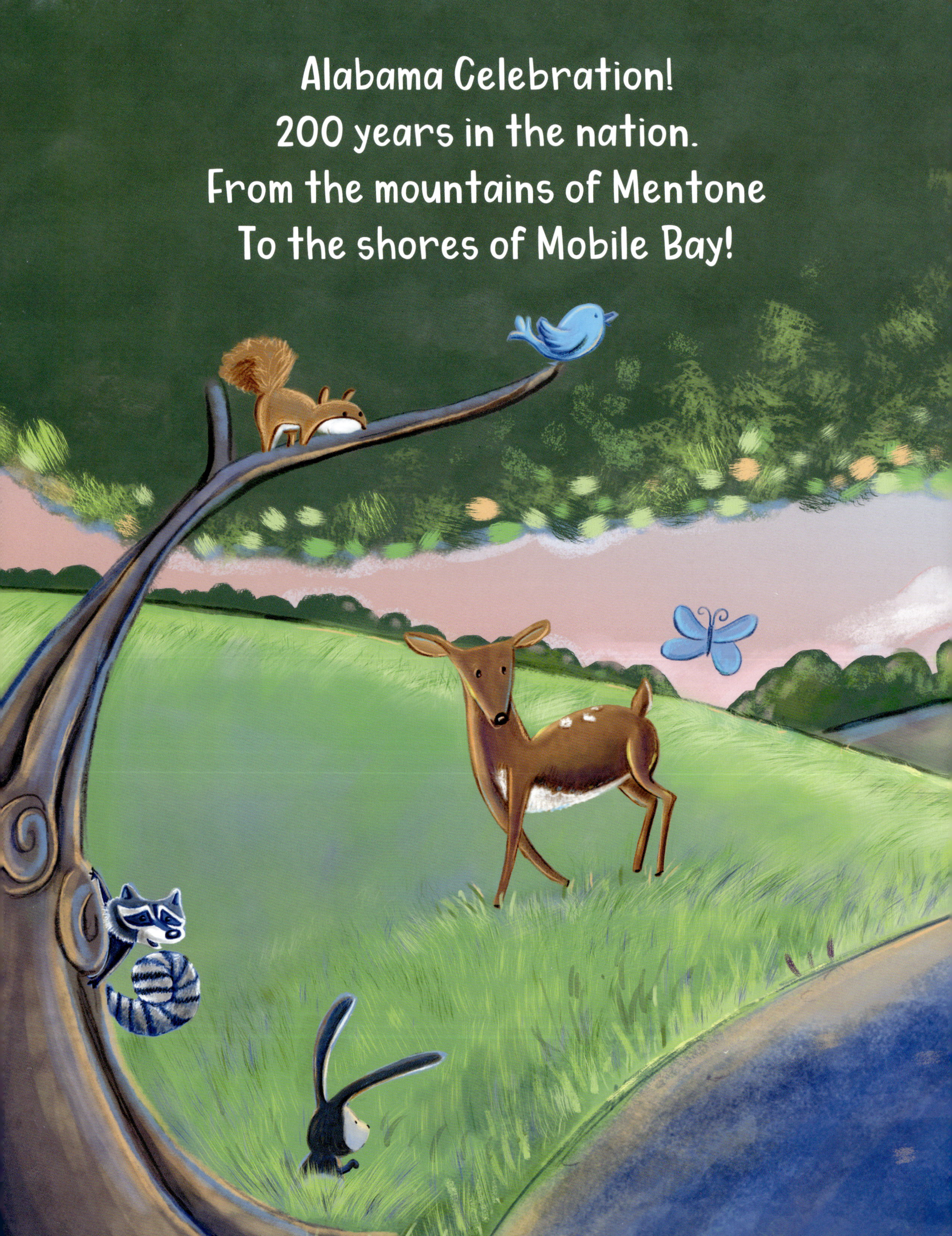

Come join the fun!
Bring everyone!
There's much to see
Along the way!

Hello! I'm Camellia!
Your bear cub guide.
I'm Alabama's mascot.
I wear our flower with pride!

So, here we go!
We're ready to roam
Across Alabama—
Our Home Sweet Home!

From North to South,
From East to West,
We're on the way—
We're on a QUEST!

To see the state
We all adore—
People, places—
And so much MORE!

Welcome to "The Rocket City!"
Huntsville is her name.
She sent a rocket to the moon
And brought our state great fame.
U.S. ARMY
SPACE CAMP
US
USA
HUNTSVILLE

Decatur is "The River City."
Oh what a beautiful place!

The birth home of Mae Jemison,
First African American
woman in space!

Helen Keller taught us how
Each challenge makes us strong.
W. C. Handy played the blues
And filled our lives with song!

Jesse Owens loved to run.
"The greatest athlete in track."
He went to the Olympics
And brought gold medals back!

Let's climb up Cheaha Mountain,
The highest in the state.
Come watch the eagles soar.
The camping here is great!
CHEAHA STATE PARK

The largest iron statue
Ever made by man,
Vulcan stands high on the hill
Watching over Birmingham.

America's Oldest Baseball Park
Is Rickwood Field in Birmingham
Where young Babe Ruth and Willie Mays
Dreamed of hitting a big grand slam!

Bo Jackson was an athlete,
"The greatest of all time."
He showed the world how legends play
When he was in his prime.

There is Coach "Bear" Bryant
With his team the Crimson Tide.
They fought their way to victory
And brought our state great pride.

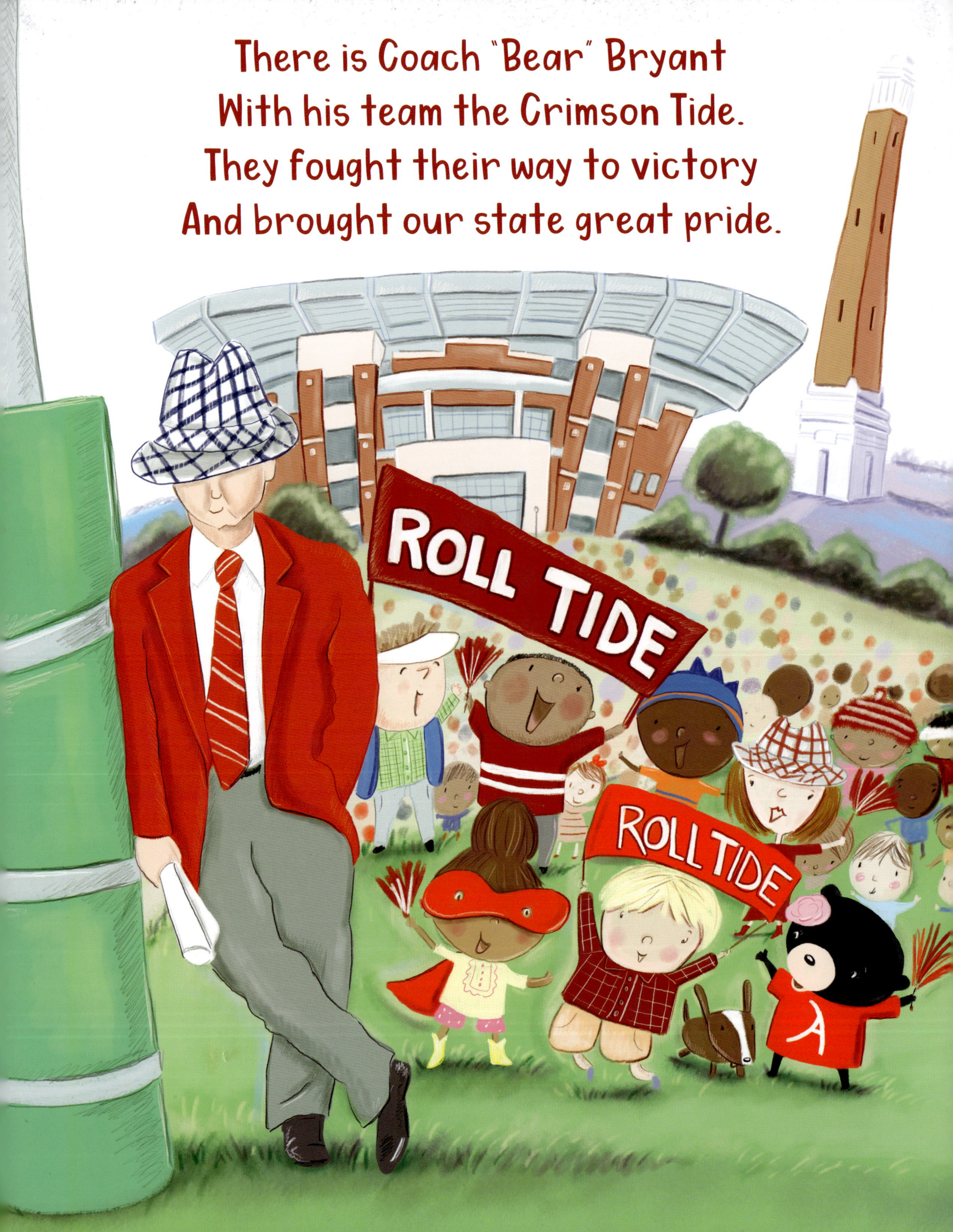

An eagle soars above the crowd
Before each game begins.
The Auburn Tigers football team
Gets ready for more wins!

The brave Airmen of Tuskegee
Fought in World War II.

George Washington Carver
Made peanuts something new!

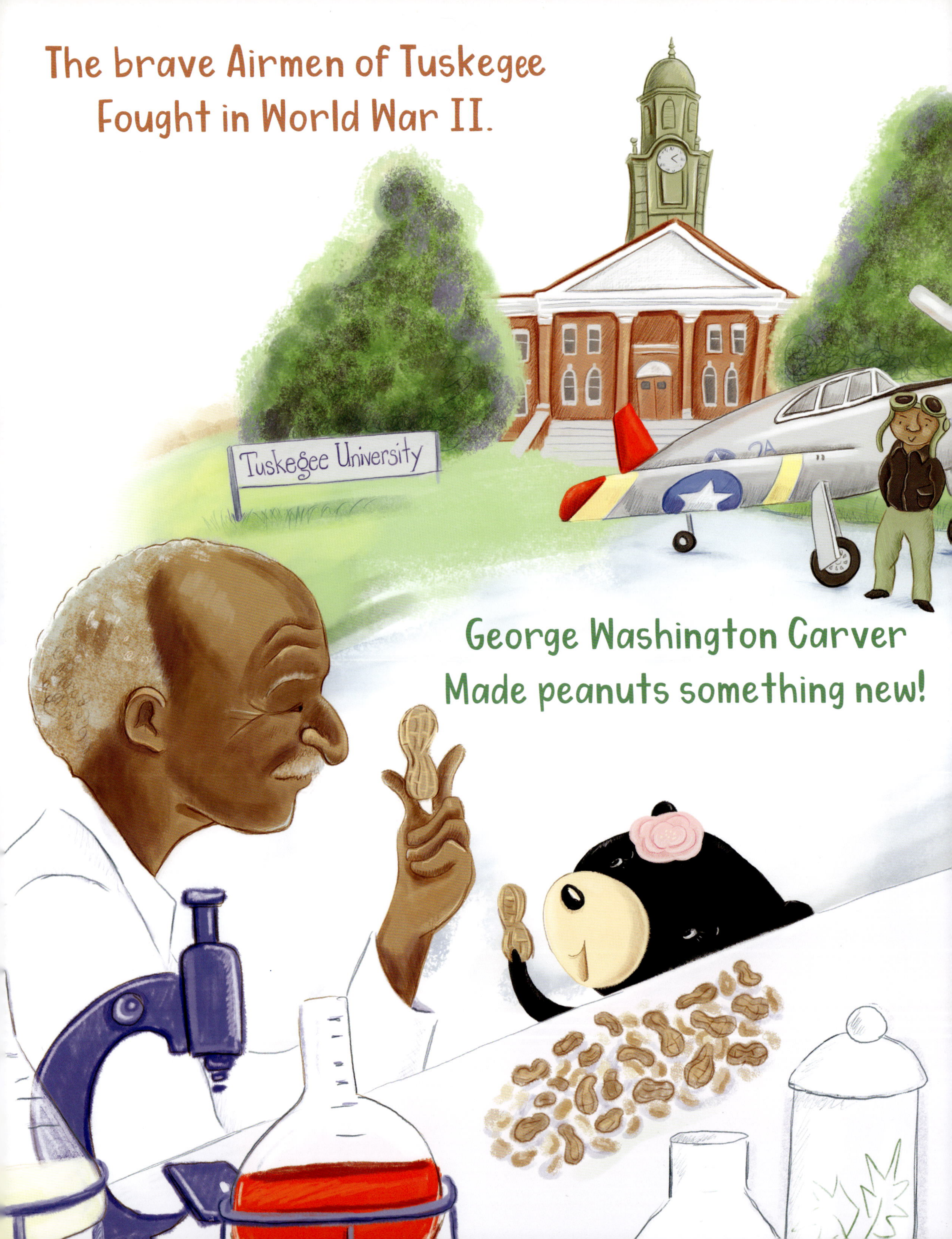

Marchers crossed the Pettus Bridge
And helped to heal our hate.

Kathryn Tucker Windham
Told stories about our state.

Native Americans called Moundville home
A thousand years ago.
They made clay pots, planted maize,
And hunted with a bow.

The dark rich soil of the Black Belt
Grew Demopolis into a town.

It sits on top of White Bluff
Where the Tombigbee River
is found.

MONTGOMERY
Who's that lady?
What's all the fuss?
It's Rosa Parks
In the front
of the bus!

There's Hank Williams
Singing his song
And Martin Luther King, Jr.
Still standing strong.

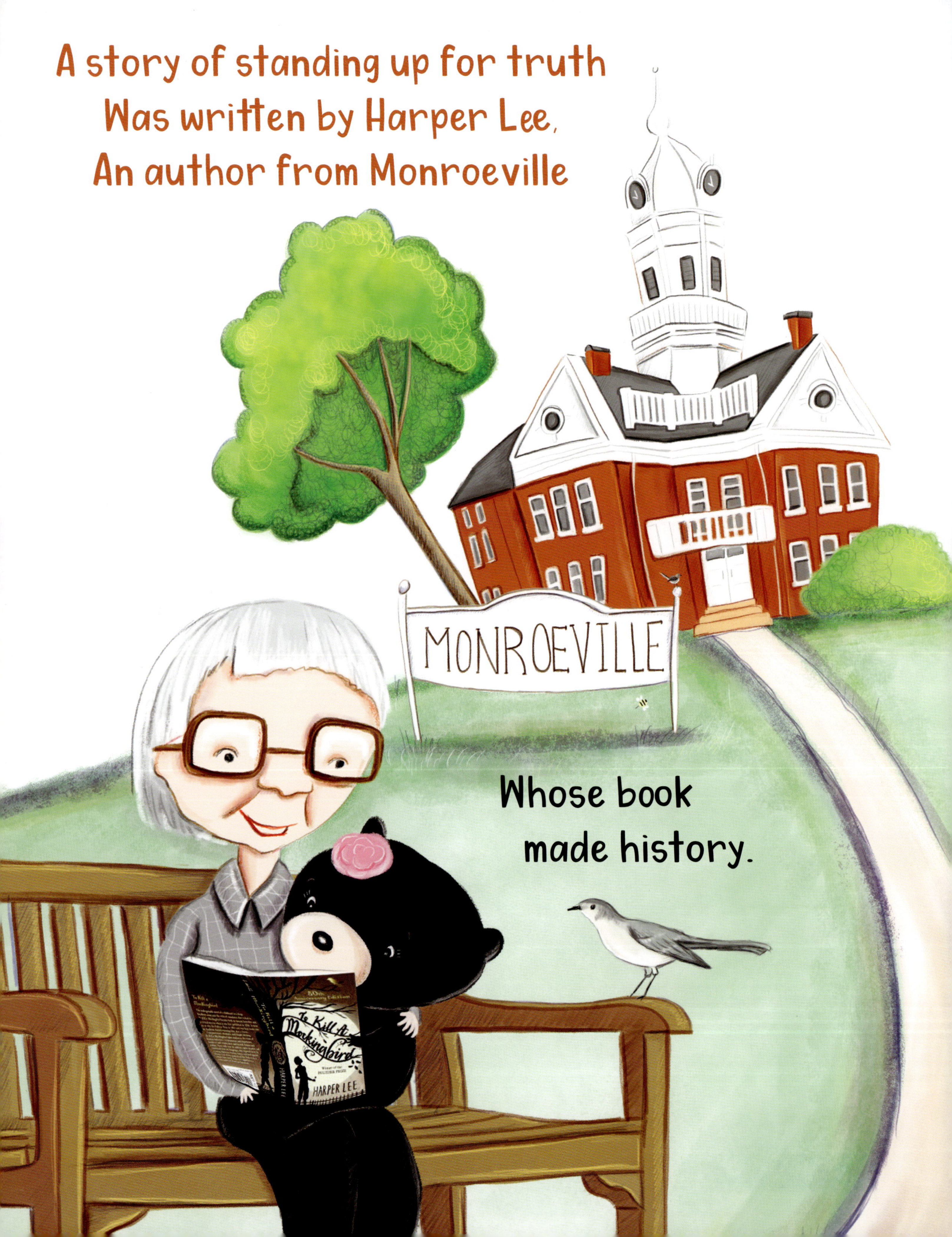

A story of standing up for truth
Was written by Harper Lee,
An author from Monroeville

Whose book
made history.

By growing lots of peanuts
Dothan earned a reputation.
This "Peanut Capital of the World"
Feeds our peanut-loving nation!

Welcome to the town of Fairhope
Where artists like to go
And every shop and sidewalk
Is putting on a show!

Here's the USS Alabama,
The battleship from World War II.
It's on display in Mobile Bay
For everyone to view!
60
MOBILE BAY

Mobile is the home of legends,
The famous pitcher Satchel Paige,
Hank Aaron, and Willie McCovey
All played in baseball's Golden Age.

Here we are at the end of our journey.
On the sugar-white sands we roam,
Playing on the beach of Gulf Shores
In Alabama — our Home Sweet Home!

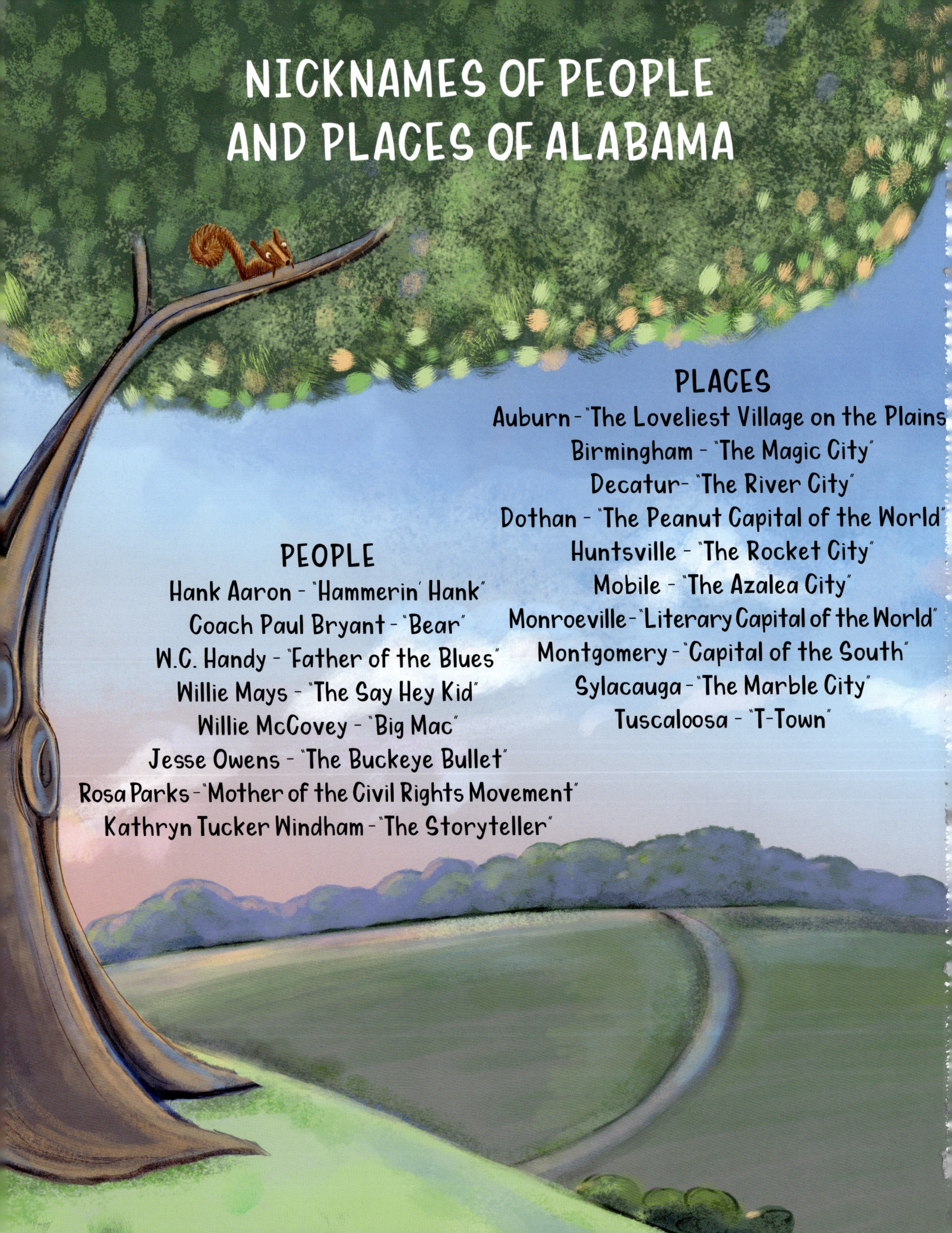

NICKNAMES OF PEOPLE AND PLACES OF ALABAMA

PLACES

Auburn - "The Loveliest Village on the Plains"
Birmingham - "The Magic City"
Decatur- "The River City"
Dothan - "The Peanut Capital of the World"
Huntsville - "The Rocket City"
Mobile - "The Azalea City"
Monroeville - "Literary Capital of the World"
Montgomery - "Capital of the South"
Sylacauga - "The Marble City"
Tuscaloosa - "T-Town"

PEOPLE

Hank Aaron - "Hammerin' Hank"
Coach Paul Bryant - "Bear"
W.C. Handy - "Father of the Blues"
Willie Mays - "The Say Hey Kid"
Willie McCovey - "Big Mac"
Jesse Owens - "The Buckeye Bullet"
Rosa Parks - "Mother of the Civil Rights Movement"
Kathryn Tucker Windham - "The Storyteller"